Copyright © 2020 by Maureen Padgett

All rights reserved. No part of this publication may be reproduced, distributed, or transmitted in any form or by any means, including photocopying, recording, or other electronic or mechanical methods, without the prior written permission of the publisher, except in the case of brief quotations embodied in critical reviews and certain other noncommercial uses permitted by copyright law

Table of Contents

The Easy Baked Mini Doughnut Cookbook: Over 40 Sweet and Delicious Recipes for Your Oven and Doughnut Maker 7

Introduction 7

Donuts Recipes 8

    Glazed Unicorn Horns 8

    Unicorn Pig Donuts 12

    Hot Chocolate Igloo Cake 19

    Mint Choc Chip Ice Cream Burger Donuts 23

    Flamingo Floatie Donuts 30

    Pineapple Upside Down Donuts 35

    Samoa Donut Ice Cream Sandwiches 38

    Hashbrown Breakfast Donuts 45

Pon de Donuts (Donut Balls) 47

Potato Doughnuts... 49

Grilled Cheese Tower 51

Carrot Cake Beignets with Chocolate Sauce .. 54

Giant Mousse Nut 56

Red Velvet Doughnuts 61

Wreath Doughnuts 67

Apple-Cranberry Cream Puff Donuts............. 70

Mini Donut Cookie Ice Cream Sandwich........ 76

4 Mini Donut Pan Hacks 79

Bacon Donuts... 81

London Fog Donuts 83

Sriracha Doughnut Holes............................. 88

Designer Donuts 90

Giant Donut 94

Golden Doughnuts 103

Homemade French Toast Balls 106

Gulab Jamun (Indian Doughnuts) 109

Chocolate-Filled Donut 113

Giant Glazed Donut Cake 116

Rainbow-Filled Doughnuts 119

Avoca-Donuts 125

Smores Freakshake Cupcakes 128

Boston Cream Donuts 137

Chocolate Samoa Cake Donuts 142

Apple Pie Donuts 146

Easy Croissant Donuts 152

Birthday Cake Baked Donuts 154

Dukkah Donuts With Blood Orange Glaze ... 158

Sun-Dried Tomato Basil Doughnuts With Cheese Filling.. 162

Monster Donuts... 167

Maple Syrup Doughnuts 172

Chocolate Strawberry Cheesecake Donuts .. 176

Apple Doughnuts....................................... 183

Nutella Cronuts 185

Lemon Meringue Donuts 187

Cinnamon Bun Doughnuts......................... 194

Tiramisu Donuts.. 198

Cat Doughnuts 203

The Easy Baked Mini Doughnut Cookbook: Over 40 Sweet and Delicious Recipes for Your Oven and Doughnut Maker

Introduction

Score baking bragging rights by perfecting how to make donuts from scratch and sharing the irresistible results. Master these irresistible fried pastries with our step-by-step instructions on how to make homemade donuts so you can enjoy them at their freshest and customize the toppings.

Donuts Recipes

Glazed Unicorn Horns

Not as mythical, but just as magical.

Ingredients

Donut Horns

- 4 cups of white flour
- 2 1/2 of tsp active dry yeast
- 3 5oz cans of evaporated milk
- 3 tbsp of butter
- 3 tbsp of sugar
- 1 tsp of salt
- 1 egg
- Vegetable oil for frying

Glaze

- 2 1/2 cups powdered sugar
- 1 tbsp melted butter
- 4 tbsp of milk
- 1 tsp of vanilla extract

Steps

Donut Horns

1. Heat the milk and butter in a small saucepan so that the butter melts - the liquid should be only slightly warm to the touch.
2. Add the yeast to the milk and let it rest for 2 minutes. Add the sugar, salt, and egg ,then whisk everything together. Finally,

add in the flour and mix with a wooden spoon to form a dough. Turn out onto a floured surface and knead for 5 minutes to form a smooth, elastic dough then place into a lightly greased bowl, cover with plastic wrap and let rise in a warm place for about 1 hour, or until doubled in size.

3. Punch down dough to deflate then place on a floured board and cut into 24 equal pieces.

4. Take one piece and roll out into a rope. Fold the rope in half so that the ends touch then twist the two strands together to form a unicorn horn. Press the ends together to seal them. Place them on a large, greased

tray and repeat the process with the rest of the dough.

5. Let the doughnuts rise for about twenty minutes.
6. While the doughnuts are resting heat the oil to 320 degrees. Fry the doughnuts in batches for about 2 minutes each side.

Glaze

1. Mix all the ingredients together in a large bowl and pour into a tall glass then dunk the doughnuts into the glass, covering them completely in the glaze. Set aside to let the glaze set slightly (if you can bear it) then serve immediately.

Unicorn Pig Donuts

Unicorns are amazing. Pigs are amazing. Donuts are amazing. Bottom line: This is amazing.

Ingredients

- Cake Donuts
- 430g (15 oz) plain (all-purpose) flour
- 265 g (91/2 oz) caster (superfine) sugar
- 3 teaspoons baking powder
- 1/2 teaspoon fine salt
- 125 g (41/2 oz/1/2 cup) unsalted butter, softened
- 2 large eggs
- 375 ml (121/2 fl oz/11/2 cups) full-cream (whole) milk

- 125 ml (4 fl oz/1/2 cup) vegetable oil
- 2 tablespoons Greek yoghurt (or sour cream)
- 1 teaspoon vanilla extract or vanilla bean paste
- 1 tsp strawberry flavouring
- 1 drop pink food gel
- Fondant Decorations
- 100g pink fondant
- 100g white fondant
- 50g black fondant
- 1 tsp gold lustre dust
- 2 tbsp vodka or vanilla extract
- 400g pink candy melts, melted
- 200g white chocolate

- ½ pastel rainbow sprinkles

Steps

1. **Fondant decorations**
2. To make the pig snouts, use a small fondant rolling pin to roll out your pink fondant on a smooth work surface to a couple mm thick. Use a 2cm round cookie cutter to cut out round discs of fondant. Use your hands to slightly flatten the top and bottom of the round disk to create an oven like shape. Use the end of a small round piping tip or a skewer to create two little nostril holes in the snout. Set aside.

3. To make the eyes, simply roll out 30 little round balls of black fondant

4. To make the unicorn corns roll out two rods of white fondant about 3cm in length. Twist them around each other. Make one end of the rod thinner and leave the other end thicker.

5. Once you have 15 of them, set them aside to dry overnig`ht. Then paint them with the gold lustre dust which you can make by combining the dust and vodka together. Let them dry for a couple hours before using. I found that make the horns is a two-day process.

6. To make the little piggy ears simply roll out 30 little balls and pinch one end to make it pointy.

7. **Donuts**

8. To make the donuts, begin by spraying a cake donut tray with cooking oil and use a pastry brush to spread around evenly. Set aside. Preheat your oven to 140C.

9. Add the flour, sugar, baking powder and salt to a large mixing bowl and mix with a hand mixer until well combined.

10. Next, add the softened butter and mix on low speed until the mixture reaches a crumbly, sand-like texture.

11. Add the eggs, milk, oil, yoghurt, pink food gel, strawberry flavoring and vanilla, and mix on low speed until all the dry ingredients are incorporated. Scrape down the side of the bowl and mix for a final 20 seconds.

12. Add to a piping bag and pipe batter into donut tray filling just over half way. Bake for 20 min and then gently tap the tray while the donuts are still warm onto a work bench. Place onto a cooling rack to cool.

13. To stick the piggy ears to the donuts, add a little dab of pink candy melts to the fondant ears and stick to the tops of your

donuts. Allow to set in the fridge for 20 min.

14. To coat the donuts place them on a cooling rack and place a baking tray underneath. Place the melted pink candy melts into a piping bag and drizzle over the donuts. Gently tap the donuts to allow the candy melts to evenly coat the donuts. You can re-use any excess candy melts on the baking tray to continue coating all of your donuts. Transfer straight from the cooling rack to a baking tray lined with baking paper to set.

15. Drizzle white chocolate on the bottom of the donuts and tap to let it settle

on the donut evenly. Sprinkle with pastel sprinkles.

16. Add a little dab of chocolate on the eyes, snout and horn and stick to the donut to finish.

Hot Chocolate Igloo Cake

It's only logical that a marshmallow covered igloo would hide a hot chocolate cake filled with chocolate ganache inside.

Ingredients

Hot Chocolate Igloo Cake

- 2 chocolate box cake mixes, prepared
- 1 packet hot chocolate mix
- 1 1/2 cups chocolate chips

Ganache and Assembly

- 1 cup heavy cream
- 1 1/2 cups chocolate chips
- 1 chocolate cake donut
- 3 cups chocolate buttercream
- 3 cups vanilla buttercream
- 8 cups mini marshmallows

Steps

Hot Chocolate Igloo Cake

1. Preheat oven to 325 degrees.
2. Grease an 8-inch glass bowl and two 8-inch cake pans and set aside.

3. Pour hot cocoa mix and chocolate chips into the cake mix. Pour into the prepared pans.
4. Bake cakes for 35 to 45 minutes or until a cake tester comes out clean.
5. Set aside to cool for 10 minutes, then invert onto a wire rack to cool completely.

Ganache and Assembly

1. Heat the heavy cream and pour it over the dark chocolate chips in a large heatproof bowl.
2. Allow mixture to sit for 5 minutes, then mix well until all chocolate is melted.

3. Cut a 3-inch round out of the center of one 8-inch cake. Set aside.
4. Build the cake by placing the bottom 8-inch round on a cake stand.
5. Ice with chocolate buttercream and top with the 8-inch round with a cut out center.
6. Level the base of the dome cake and place on top.
7. Using a funnel, poke a hole through the top of your igloo.
8. Ice the outside of the cake with chocolate buttercream, place a donut on one side as a door, ice it and place in the refrigerator to set.

9. Once the cake is set, coat the cake with vanilla buttercream.

10. Using mini marshmallows, cover the whole cake in an igloo ice cube pattern.

11. Fill with the warm ganache, and serve immediately.

Mint Choc Chip Ice Cream Burger Donuts

Ice cream sandwiches are played out... Introducing the ice cream burger!

Ingredients

Mint Chocolate Chip Ice Cream

- 1 ½ cups thickened/whipping cream
- ½ cup sweetened condensed milk
- 1 tsp vanilla extract

- 1 tsp peppermint
- 2 drops teal food gel
- 1 mini choc chips

Donuts

- 2 1/4 tsp active dry yeast
- 1/2 cup warm water, 110 degrees
- 1/4 cup granulated sugar
- 1/4 cup evaporated milk, warmed to 110 degrees
- 1/2 tsp salt
- 1/4 cup melted butter
- 1 large egg
- 1 egg yolk

- 1/2 tsp vanilla extract
- 420g 2 1/2 cups all-purpose flour, then more as needed
- 1 cup cinnamon sugar
- 3 - 4 cups vegetable oil, for frying

Decorations

- Chocolate sauce to drizzle
- Funfetti sprinkles

Steps

Mint Chocolate Chip Ice Cream

1. Add cream, powdered sugar, peppermint extract, green food gel and vanilla extract into a large mixing bowl and whip to stiff peaks using a hand mixer.

2. Add chocolate chips and fold in.
3. Add to a rectangle baking tin lined with plastic wrap and flatten out using a spatula.
4. Cover with plastic wrap and freeze overnight or for 4 hours.
5. Use a 3 inch cookie cutter to cut out disks of the ice cream.
6. Transfer to a serving platter or baking tray and place in the freezer until ready to use.

Donuts

1. In a small bowl, whisk together yeast, warm water and 1/2 tsp of the sugar.

2. Cover it with cling wrap and a towel. Let it rest 5 - 10 minutes in a warm spot until it becomes frothy.

3. Add in yeast mixture, milk, remaining granulated sugar, salt, melted butter, egg, egg yolk and vanilla.

4. Add half of the flour and set mixer with whisk attachment and blend until smooth.

5. Switch mixer to hook attachment, slowly add remaining flour and knead on low speed until smooth and elastic about 4 - 5 minutes, adding additional flour as needed (I only added about 2 Tbsp more. You shouldn't need a lot more, you want dough

to be slightly sticky and tacky but shouldn't stick to a clean fingertip).

6. Transfer dough to a lightly oiled bowl, cover with plastic wrap and let rise in a warm place until double in size, about 1 1/2 hours.
7. Roll dough into an even layer onto a floured surface to slightly less than 1/2-inch thickness.
8. Cut into doughnut shapes using a 3 inch cookie cutter.
9. Cover with a clean tea towel and let them rise in a warm spot until doubled, about 30 - 40 minutes.

10. Preheat the oil in a large pot on medium high heat. Drop a small amount of dough into the oil and if it bubbles and fizzes around the sides the oil is hot enough. Gently and carefully drop donuts into the oil. Don't add more than three donuts at a time. Cook them on one side until they're a light golden brown then flip them over.

11. Once they're golden on both sides carefully take them out and transfer them to a plate lined with kitchen paper towels to let the oil drain.

12. Roll the donuts around in the cinnamon sugar while they're still warm.

13. Set aside.

14. Slice the donuts in half and add an ice cream disk.

Decorations

1. Drizzle with chocolate sauce and finish with sprinkles.

2. Donuts are best served the day they're made.

Flamingo Floatie Donuts

Let me float this delicious idea by you: flamingo pool floatie donuts!

Ingredients

- Cake
- 429g all-purpose flour

- 265g caster (superfine) sugar
- 3 tsp baking powder
- 1/2 tsp salt
- 125g unsalted butter, softened
- 2 large eggs
- 375ml of milk
- 125ml vegetable oil
- 2 tbsp Greek yogurt
- 1 tsp pineapple flavouring
- 2 drops teal food gel

- **Decorations**

  - 300g pink candy melts, melted
  - 12 yellow mini m&m candies
  - 50g dark chocolate, melted

- 500g pink fondant

Steps

1. Necks, wings and tails.
2. To make the tails and wings, roll out some fondant to about 1cm thick. Use a 3cm round cookie cutter to cut out 36 circles. Use your fingers to pinch one side of the circles.
3. To make the necks roll out a ball of fondant about the size of a teaspoon and then roll out into a log about 10cm in length. Shaped into a question mark shape and allow to dry for 4 hours.

4. Add some melted dark chocolate to the tip of the fondant shape and allow to set.
5. Use the small yellow candies to make an indent into the tops of the shape, add some dark chocolate and stick the yellow candy to the fondant. Set aside.
6. Cake
7. Preheat a fan-forced oven to 140C (280F) or 160C (320F) for a conventional oven. Spray a cake donut tin with oil and set aside.
8. Add the flour, sugar, baking powder and salt to a large mixing bowl and mix together using a hand mixer to combine.

9. Next add the softened butter and mix on low speed until mixture reaches a crumbly sand like texture.

10. Add the eggs, milk, oil, Greek yogurt and pineapple flavouring. Mix on low speed until no dry ingredients are showing. Scrape down the bowl and mix for a final 20 seconds. Add the teal food gel and set aside.

11. Add the batter to a piping bag and pipe into the donuts tray filling each hole just above half way. Bake for 20 minutes and allow to cool completely.

12. Dip the tops of the donuts into melted pink candy melts. Stick two wings

to each side of the donut and a wing shape on the back of the donut for the tail.

13. Stick the necks in some melted pink candy melts and stick to the top of the donuts to finish.

Pineapple Upside Down Donuts

Now this is a story all about how these pineapple donuts got flipped upside down...

Ingredients

- 1 large egg
- 1/3 cup light brown sugar, plus more for sprinkling
- 2 tablespoons whole milk

- 2 tablespoons fresh pineapple juice
- 1/4 cup sour cream
- 2 tablespoons unsalted butter, melted
- 1 1/2 teaspoons vanilla extract
- 1 cup self-rising flour
- 1 (15-ounce) can of pineapple rings
- Maraschino cherries, for garnish

Steps

1. Preheat oven to 350 degrees.
2. Spray a donut pan with nonstick cooking spray.
3. In a medium bowl, whisk together egg, brown sugar, milk, pineapple juice, sour cream, melted butter, and vanilla extract.

4. Gently add in the self-rising flour until combined.
5. In each well of the donut pan, sprinkle about 1 tablespoon of brown sugar and lay half a pineapple ring (sliced in half lengthwise so the cake/fruit ratio is even).
6. Carefully spoon the batter over the pineapple rings and spread evenly.
7. Bake for 15 to 20 minutes.
8. Set aside to cool on a wire rack.
9. Turn the pan upside down to flip the donuts out.
10. Garnish each with a cherry in the middle, serve and enjoy!

Samoa Donut Ice Cream Sandwiches

These are appropriate for breakfast since they have donuts in them, right?

Ingredients

Donuts

- 1 stick (1/2 cup) plus 2 tablespoons butter, softened
- 1 cup sugar
- 2 large eggs
- 3 cups all-purpose flour

- 4 teaspoons baking powder
- 1/2 teaspoon salt
- 1 cup whole milk

Caramel Icing

- 2 cups light brown sugar
- 1/4 cup (1/2 stick) unsalted butter
- 1/3 cup heavy cream
- 1/3 cup powdered sugar

To Assemble

- 1 1/2 cups coconut flakes
- 1 cup semisweet chocolate, finely chopped
- 1 tablespoon coconut oil
- 2 pints vanilla ice cream (in their cartons)

Steps

Donuts

1. Preheat oven to 350 degrees.
2. Grease two 6-cavity donut pans with butter or nonstick cooking spray.
3. In a large mixing bowl, cream together butter and sugar.
4. Add the eggs and beat until well mixed.
5. In a separate bowl, sift together the flour, baking powder and salt.
6. With beater on low, add to the butter and sugar mixture until just mixed.
7. Add the milk and mix well.

8. Fill greased donut pans two-thirds of the way with batter.

9. Bake for 15 to 20 minutes, or until donuts are golden brown. Remove from oven and let cool fully.

Caramel Icing

1. Immediately before you ice the donuts, make the icing.

2. In a medium saucepan over medium heat, melt butter and brown sugar.

3. Stir in cream and let mixture caramelize for 5 to 7 minutes.

4. Add powdered sugar and whisk until smooth. Let mixture continue heating until

thick enough to coat the back of a wooden spoon or spatula. If it starts to dry up, quickly reheat on the stove or in the microwave.

To Assemble

1. Chill a large parchment-lined baking sheet, and have your caramel, chocolate and coconut nearby.
2. In a large pan over medium heat, toast the shredded coconut until golden brown. Watch carefully and stir often so it doesn't burn.
3. In a medium microwavable bowl, place the chopped chocolate and coconut oil. Heat in

microwave, stirring every 15 seconds, until melted.

4. Dip the bottom half of each doughnut in the melted chocolate.

5. Place the donut chocolate side down onto the chilled cookie sheet. Place in the freezer for about 5 minutes or until chocolate is set. Remove from freezer and dip the tops of the donuts in the caramel icing.

6. Immediately dip into the toasted coconut flakes.

7. Place donut back on baking sheet chocolate side down.

8. Drizzle the remaining melted chocolate over each donut in lines.//
9. Use a pastry bag for cleaner lines.
10. Chill in the freezer until firm.
11. Cut chilled donuts in half widthwise.
12. Using a serrated knife, cut slices out of the pints of ice cream starting from the bottom of the carton.
13. Place an ice cream slice on the bottom of a donut half and top with the caramel coconut half. Peel off paper. Alternatively, you can scoop ice cream onto the half directly, and gently flatten the ice cream. Keep in the freezer in an airtight container for 1 week.

Hashbrown Breakfast Donuts

Like delightful breakfast bundt cakes, these hashbrown breakfast donuts will have you jumping out of bed!

Ingredients

- 2 large russet potatoes, shredded
- 2 cups cheddar cheese, shredded
- 1/2 cup bacon, cooked and chopped
- 1/2 cup green onion, chopped
- 1 tablespoon olive oil
- 2 teaspoons salt
- 2 teaspoons pepper
- 6 eggs, poached
- 1/2 cup queso sauce

- 2 tablespoons parsley, minced

Steps

1. Preheat oven to 400 degrees.
2. Spray donut pan with cooking spray.
3. In a large bowl, add potatoes, cheese, bacon, green onions, olive oil, salt and pepper. Mix until combined.
4. Fill each donut hole with mixture, filling it up to the top and pressing it in.
5. Bake 15 to 20 minutes until golden brown.
6. Top with poached egg, queso and parsley.

Pon de Donuts (Donut Balls)

Since these delicious, chewy-on-the-inside donuts are made out of tofu, that technically makes them health food, right?

Ingredients

- 7 ounces silky tofu
- 1 cup cake flour
- 1 cup rice flour
- 1 1/2 teaspoons baking powder
- 5 tablespoons sugar
- Cooking oil
- Honey glaze:
- 1 cup powdered sugar
- 1 tablespoon honey

- 1 tablespoon milk

Steps

1. Mash the silky tofu through a strainer into a mixing bowl. Add the rice flour, cake flour, baking powder and sugar. Mix well.

2. Heat a deep-sided pot of cooking oil to 350 degrees.

3. Roll the dough into bite-sized pieces. On a square of parchment paper, arrange 7 balls to form a circle. Place the entire paper with the dough balls into the hot oil. Fry on one side, then flip and remove parchment paper. Continue frying until golden brown.

4. In a small bowl, combine ingredients for honey glaze. Drizzle over doughnuts, and enjoy.

Potato Doughnuts

Filled with potatoes along with mozzarella and cheddar cheeses, these flavor-packed savory doughnuts pair perfectly with marinara sauce.

Ingredients

- 12 ounces potatoes, divided
- 1/4 cup shredded mozzarella cheese
- 1/4 cup cheddar cheese, cubed
- 1/4 cup heavy cream
- 2 tablespoons chestnut flour/powder
- Salt and pepper

- Wheat flour
- 3 eggs, beaten
- Breadcrumbs
- Oil, for frying
- Tomato sauce

Steps

1. Cook half of the potatoes, allow to cool then mash. Slice the other half into thin strips.
2. In a mixing bowl, add both kinds of potato, chestnut powder, salt, pepper, cheese and heavy cream. Stir to combine.

3. Divide the mixture among the openings of a donut pan, pressing down to flatten. Place in the refrigerator to firm up.
4. Add flour to one shallow dish, eggs to a second dish, and breadcrumbs to a third. Dip each potato donut first in the flour then in the eggs and finally in the breadcrumbs.
5. In a high-sided pan, heat oil to 350 degrees. Carefully submerge donuts in the hot oil and cook until light brown. Serve with tomato sauce.

Grilled Cheese Tower

There's no such thing as too much grilled cheese or too many donuts, so why not pile them high with slabs of bacon in between?

Ingredients

- 24 slices bacon
- 6 glazed doughnuts, sliced in half
- 12 slices Swiss cheese
- 12 slices American cheese
- 1 skewer
- 1 small cube of cheese

Steps

1. In a cast-iron pan, cook bacon until crispy. Remove bacon to a paper-towel lined plate, leaving the rendered bacon fat in the pan.
2. Reduce heat to medium-low and add doughnut halves, insides facing down.

Place one slice of each kind of cheese on top of half of the doughnut halves.

3. Allow doughnuts to toast and cheese to melt, then top cheese-covered doughnuts with the plain ones and remove from pan. Continue with remaining doughnuts and cheese.
4. Insert a skewer into a small cube of cheese and stand up on a plate. Add one doughnut sandwich, followed by a layer of bacon.
5. Continue alternating doughnut sandwiches and bacon, ending with a doughnut sandwich on top.

Carrot Cake Beignets with Chocolate Sauce

Better your beignet game with this carrot cake variety paired with a sweet chocolate sauce.

Ingredients

- 2 small carrots, chopped
- 2 eggs
- 1 tablespoon cooking oil
- 1/2 cup sugar
- 1/2 cup milk
- 2 1/2 cups wheat flour
- 1 teaspoon cachaça
- Orange zest, to taste
- 1 teaspoon baking powder

- Oil for frying
- 1/2 cup powdered sugar
- 1 teaspoon cinnamon
- 5 ounces dark chocolate
- 1 cup heavy cream

Steps

1. In a blender, beat the carrots, eggs, oil, sugar and milk.
2. Transfer to a bowl, and gradually add the wheat flour until the mixture reaches the ideal consistency. Add the cachaça, orange zest and baking powder, and mix. Using a spoon, place portions of the dough in the hot oil. Brown on both sides and drain on

paper towels. Toss the cakes in a mixture of sugar and cinnamon.

3. In a double-boiler, melt the chocolate with the heavy cream until a smooth sauce is obtained. Serve the cakes with the chocolate sauce.

Giant Mousse Nut

What looks like an artfully decorated frosted donut is actually a white chocolate shell filled with rich chocolate mousse.

Ingredients

- Moussenut shell
- 600g white chocolate
- 100g red chocolate melts

- Mousse
- 2 tbsp butter
- 12 ounces dark chocolate
- 1 ¾ cup whipping cream
- 2 tbsp powdered gelatin
- 4 tbsp water

Steps

1. Moussenut shell
2. To make chocolate shell melt white chocolate in a large microwave safe bowl for 20 seconds at a time mixing each time until smooth. The key is to go slow otherwise you risk burning the chocolate. Repeat with the red choc melts. Allow both

to cool slightly before using. By the way, you can use any colour combinations you like! Dark choc and white choc, green and red, anything! :0)

3. Add red choc melts to a piping bag and drizzle squiggly lines on the inside of a donut mould. The mould I used is called a Pavoflex Galaxy Silicone Mould. It measures 175mm x 55mm and holds 100ml. Allow to chill for 10 min before you pour the white chocolate in. Swirl it around to get the chocolate to cover all the inside. You may want to gently use the back of a spoon to help the chocolate cover everything. Once you've done that, turn it

upside down onto a baking tray and allow any excess white chocolate to drip out before you chill for 25 min.

4. It takes a bit of convincing to get the chocolate out of the mould. If you feel like your layer of chocolate is too thin and won't be strong enough to come out of the mould add a second layer of white chocolate.

5. Mousse

6. Add chocolate and butter into a microwave safe bowl and microwave for 20 seconds at a time, mixing each time until smooth. Allow to cool slightly.

7. Add water and gelatine into a mixing bowl. Mix together. Allow to sit for 5 minutes before you microwave for 10 seconds to melt slightly.

8. Add to chocolate mixture and mix in well. Set aside to cool slightly, but don't allow it to set with that chocolate in there.

9. Add cream into a large mixing bowl and whip to stiff peaks. Add a spatula full of the cream to the chocolate mixture and fold in. Then add the rest of the cream and fold in.

10. Add the mousse into the chocolate shell and chill for 2 hours to allow to set.

11. To serve run a knife under hot water and cut through the shell and mousse to cut out your servings.

Red Velvet Doughnuts

These delicious red velvet fried doughnuts are topped with glaze and stuffed full of cream cheese filling!

Ingredients

Red Velvet Doughnuts

- 2 tbsp active dry yeast
- ½ cup warm water
- 1 tsp granulated sugar
- 2 ½ cups all-purpose flour
- ¼ cup granulated sugar

- 2 large eggs
- 2 tbsp red food coloring
- 2 tbsp unsalted butter, room temperature
- 2 tsp salt
- ½ cup mini chocolate chips
- canola oil

Filling

- 125g cream cheese, room temperature
- ¾ cup unsalted butter, room temperature
- 1 ¼ cups confectioner's sugar
- ½ tsp vanilla extract

Glaze

- 1 ½ cups confectioner's sugar

- ½ cup whipping cream

Steps

Red Velvet Doughnuts

1. Place the yeast, warm water and 1 tsp granulated sugar into the bowl of an electric mixer fitted with the dough hook attachment. Allow this to sit for 10 minutes, until the yeast begins to develop.
2. Add the flour, ¼ cup sugar, eggs, red food coloring, butter and salt. Set the mixer to medium speed and knead for 8-9 minutes, until the dough is smooth, soft and bounces back when poked with your finger.

3. Add the mini chocolate chips and knead until incorporated. Place the dough in an oiled bowl and cover with plastic wrap. Place in a warm spot until doubled in size, about 1 hour.
4. Roll the dough out to ¼ inch-thick and cut into 2 ½ inch-wide circles with a cookie cutter. You should be able to get 15-20 doughnuts.
5. Transfer the doughnuts to a lightly floured baking sheet and cover with a sheet of plastic wrap. Place in a warm spot and let rise for 20 minutes.
6. Pour about 5 inches of canola oil into a pot and set to medium heat. Attach a deep-fry

thermometer and heat the oil to 370F. Fry 3 or 4 doughnuts at a time, cooking for 1 minute on each side or until golden.

7. Remove the doughnuts from the oil with a slotted spoon and place on a baking sheet lined with paper towel. Cool completely.

8. Poke holes into the sides of the doughnuts with a knife. Fill the doughnuts with the filling.

9. Dunk the doughnuts into the glaze, then place on a wire rack. Allow the glaze to set and enjoy!

Filling

1. Beat the cream cheese and butter with an electric mixer until pale and fluffy.
2. Add the vanilla extract and beat until combined.
3. Add the confectioner's sugar one cup at a time, then beat well. Place in a piping bag fitted with a large, round piping tip.

Glaze

1. Combine the confectioner's sugar and whipping cream in a bowl.

Wreath Doughnuts

Baked vanilla doughnuts come with an extra helping of holiday cheer (i.e., frosting) in the form of festive wreaths!

Ingredients

- **Doughnut Batter:**

  - 1 cup all-purpose flour
  - 1 tsp baking powder
  - ¼ tsp salt
  - 3 tbsp unsalted butter, melted
  - ¼ cup sugar
  - 2 tbsp honey
  - 1 large egg
  - 1 tsp vanilla extract

- 1/3 cup + 1 tbsp buttermilk
- green food coloring

- **Frosting:**

  - 1 cup unsalted butter, room temperature
  - dash vanilla extract
  - 2 1/2 cups confectioner's sugar
  - red and green food coloring
  - Holiday sprinkles

Steps

1. Whisk together the flour, baking powder and salt in a small bowl and set aside. In a large bowl, combine the butter, sugar, honey, egg and vanilla extract. Add the buttermilk and mix until combined. Add the

dry ingredients and mix until just combined – make sure not to overmix. Dye the batter green with the food coloring.

2. Spoon the batter into a piping bag, then pipe the batter into a greased doughnut pan and bake at 400F for 7 minutes. Cool for 1 minute in the pan, then flip the pan over to remove the doughnuts and cool completely on a wire rack.

3. Beat the butter with an electric mixer at room temperature until light and fluffy. Add the vanilla extract and beat until combined. Add the confectioner's sugar one cup at a time, then beat for 3 minutes, until fluffy.

Dye ¼ cup of the frosting red and the remaining frosting green.

4. Place the red frosting into a piping bag fitted with a small, round piping tip. Place the green frosting into a piping bag fitted with a small, star-shaped piping tip.

5. Pipe the green frosting onto the doughnuts to look like pine needles and create a bow with the red frosting. Decorate with holiday sprinkles and enjoy!

Apple-Cranberry Cream Puff Donuts

Take a sweet bite of the holiday season with flaky pumpkin-spiced cream puffs filled with an apple-cranberry compote and whipped cream.

Ingredients

Apple-Cranberry Compote

- 3 Honeycrisp apples, peeled, cored and diced
- 6 ounces fresh cranberries
- 1/2 cup granulated sugar
- 1 teaspoon vanilla extract
- 1 slice fresh orange peel
- 1 orange, juiced
- 1/2 teaspoon pumpkin pie spice
- 1 pinch kosher salt

Cream Puff Donuts

- 1 cup water

- 8 tablespoons unsalted butter, room temperature
- 3 teaspoons granulated sugar
- 1 teaspoon pumpkin pie spice
- 1 cup all-purpose flour
- 4 large eggs

Whipped Cream

- 2/3 cup heavy whipping cream
- 1 tablespoon powdered sugar
- Powdered sugar, for dusting

Steps

Apple-Cranberry Compote

1. To make the compote: In a medium saucepan over medium heat, add all of the

ingredients. Bring to a boil and reduce to a simmer to cook for 20 minutes until the apples and cranberries are broken down.
2. Remove from heat to cool completely.
3. Discard the orange peel.
4. Refrigerate compote until ready to use.

Cream Puff Donuts

1. To make the donuts: Place oven rack in the center, and preheat oven 375 degrees.
2. In a medium saucepan over medium heat, add 1 cup of water, the butter, sugar and pumpkin pie spice. Whisk to combine.
3. Using a wooden spoon, briskly stir the flour into the liquid until a dough forms.

Continue to stir the dough for 1 to 2 minutes.

4. Turn off the heat and transfer the dough into the bowl of a stand mixer fitted with the paddle attachment. Mix the dough on low-medium speed.
5. Then add 1 egg at a time, mixing until incorporated and increasing the speed with each addition until the dough is sticky and glossy.
6. Pour the dough into a large (18-inch) piping bag fitted with a small star tip.
7. Pipe the dough into the mini donut pans, filling only halfway (the cream puffs will rise while baking).

8. Place onto a baking sheet to keep the pans level in the oven, and bake on the center rack for 30 to 35 minutes until puffed, crusty on the outside and lightly golden brown.

9. Cool in the pan for 5 minutes before removing to a cooling rack.

10. Bake the remaining dough.

Whipped Cream

1. To make the whipped cream: Pour the whipping cream into a large mixing bowl. Using a hand mixer fitted with beaters, whisk the cream to soft peaks. Add the powdered sugar and beat to stiff peaks.

2. To assemble the cream puff donuts: Cut each donut in half crosswise.

3. Put 1 tablespoon of compote on the bottom half.

4. Top with a dollop of whipped cream, then finish with the donut top.

5. To serve, dust the donuts with powdered sugar.

6. Best served fresh, but leftovers can be stored in the refrigerator for up to 3 days.

Mini Donut Cookie Ice Cream Sandwich

A mini donut pan opens the world to endless dessert possibilities like these cookie ice cream sandwiches dipped in chocolate.

Ingredients

- 1 stick unsalted butter, melted
- 1/2 cup brown sugar
- 1/4 cup white sugar
- 1 large egg
- 1/2 teaspoon pure vanilla extract
- 1 cup all¬-purpose flour
- 1/4 teaspoon baking soda
- 1/2 teaspoon fine salt
- 5 ounces mini chocolate chips
- 1 (4-ounce) bar semisweet chocolate
- 1 1/2 tablespoons coconut oil
- 2 cups vanilla ice cream, softened
- Flaky sea salt

Steps

1. Preheat oven to 350 degrees. Spray the mini doughnut pan with nonstick spray.
2. In a large bowl, whisk the melted butter, sugars, egg and vanilla until smooth.
3. In a separate bowl, combine the flour, baking soda and salt.
4. Stir the dry ingredients into the wet ingredients. Fold in the chocolate chips.
5. Fill each cavity of the mini doughnut pan with chocolate chip dough and bake for 12 minutes. Remove and let cool.
6. In a double boiler, melt chocolate and coconut oil together.

7. Place about 2 tablespoons of softened vanilla ice cream on top of half of the cookie doughnuts. Top each with another cookie. Dip top cookie into melted chocolate and sprinkle with sea salt. Freeze to set.

4 Mini Donut Pan Hacks

Donut underestimate the number of uses a mini donut pan offers.

- Crayons
- Piñata Cakes
- Egg Sandwiches
- Bird Feeders

Ingredients

- 1 cup water
- 3 tablespoons agar agar
- 1 tablespoon honey
- 1 1/2 cups bird seed

Steps

1. Bring water to a boil. Stir in agar agar and honey until dissolved. Transfer to a large bowl along with bird seed and stir to combine.
2. Fill each cavity of the mini doughnut pan with bird seed mixture. Refrigerate to set. Tie with decorative ribbon.

Bacon Donuts

Sure to satisfy those sweet and savory cravings, this bacon donut comes stuffed with an onion ring, pineapple ring and filled with mozzarella cheese.

Ingredients

- 12 thick pineapple slices
- 12 onion rings, 1/2 inch thick
- 6 mozzarella cheese sticks
- 36 strips bacon
- 1 cup barbecue sauce

Steps

1. Line a baking sheet with parchment paper, and preheat the oven to 350 degrees.
2. Place a pineapple ring inside each onion ring, trimming the pineapple if necessary. Split a cheese stick in half and wrap around the inside of the onion ring. Wrap 3 pieces of bacon around pineapple onion ring, through the center hole and around the outside until the entire pineapple is covered. Repeat these steps until all pineapple slices are used.
3. Place donuts on lined baking sheet and brush with barbecue sauce. Bake for 10 to 12 minutes until bacon is cooked.

4. Remove from oven and brush again with sauce. Serve warm.

London Fog Donuts

Make donut time into tea time (or vice versa) with these baked donuts infused with Earl Grey tea. Cheerio!

Ingredients

London Fog Donuts

- 4 eggs
- 1/4 cup coconut oil, melted
- 1/4 cup maple syrup
- 1/4 cup + 2 tablespoons brewed Earl Grey tea (brewed in coconut milk)
- 1 teaspoon vanilla extract

- 1 cup almond flour
- 1/2 cup coconut flour
- 1 tablespoon coconut sugar
- 1 teaspoon lemon zest
- 1 1/2 teaspoons baking powder
- 1/4 teaspoon baking soda
- 1/2 teaspoon sea salt

Glaze

- 4 tablespoons coconut butter
- 3 teaspoons coconut sugar
- 2 teaspoons maple syrup
- 1/2 lemon, juiced
- 1 teaspoon vanilla extract

- Earl Grey tea, to thin (brewed in coconut milk)
- 3 drops purple food coloring
- Lemon zest

Steps

London Fog Donuts

1. For the donuts: Preheat oven to 350 degrees.
2. In a medium bowl, whisk together the eggs, coconut oil, maple syrup, Earl Grey tea and vanilla extract.
3. In a separate bowl, combine the flours, coconut sugar, lemon zest, baking powder, baking soda and sea salt.

4. Add the wet ingredients to the dry ingredients and mix to combine.
5. Transfer the mixture to a large zip-top plastic bag. Make a medium-sized cut on one corner of the bag.
6. Grease the donut tins with coconut oil and pipe in the batter.
7. Gently tap the batter down with your fingers so the dough is even.
8. Place in oven and bake for 20 to 25 minutes, until tops are golden brown and firm to the touch.

Glaze

1. For the glaze: Melt coconut butter in the microwave until it becomes a smooth liquid.
2. Add the coconut sugar, maple syrup, vanilla extract, and whisk to combine.
3. Slowly add the Earl Grey tea to thin out glaze mixture.
4. Add food coloring and stir to combine.
5. Lastly, add the lemon juice and stir to combine.
6. Dip cooled donuts in glaze.
7. Sprinkle with lemon zest before serving.

Sriracha Doughnut Holes

These quick and easy donut holes have just the right kick of Sriracha spice to go along with their sweetness.

Ingredients

Maple and Sriracha Glaze

- 1 cup powdered sugar
- 1/2 cup maple syrup
- 2 tablespoons Sriracha

Donuts Balls

- 1 can pre-made regular biscuit dough
- Oil, for frying

Steps

Maple and Sriracha Glaze

1. In a mixing bowl, whisk together the powdered sugar, maple syrup and Sriracha until it forms a smooth glaze.

Donuts Balls

1. In a deep-sided pot over medium heat, preheat oil to 350 degrees.
2. Separate the biscuits and cut into quarters. Roll each quarter into a little ball.
3. Fry balls until golden brown, about 1 to 2 minutes, in small batches. Use tongs to make sure they fry evenly.
4. Transfer donut balls to a cooling rack.

5. While the donuts are warm, pour the glaze over top.

Designer Donuts

Get fancy with trendy chocolate donuts covered in chocolate frosting on top of a cone filled with chocolate buttercream batter.

Ingredients

- 50g cocoa powder
- 175g all-purpose flour
- ½ tsp salt
- ½ tsp bicarbonate of soda
- 225g caster sugar
- 175g unsalted butter, softened
- 2 large eggs, at room temperature

- 1 tsp vanilla extract
- 175ml milk
- 6 ice cream waffle cones
- 3 tbsp vanilla buttercream frosting
- 200g pink chocolate melts (melted)
- 200g blue chocolate melts (melted)
- 400g white chocolate melts (melted)

Steps

1. Preheat a fan-forced oven to 160C (320F) or 180C (356F) for a conventional oven. Line a baking tray with baking paper. Spray a donut baking tray with oil and set aside.
2. In the bowl of a stand mixer fitted with the paddle attachment, add the cocoa powder,

plain flour, salt, bicarb soda and sugar. Turn mixer on low speed and allow it to mix for a couple minutes to help everything combine well! (alternatively you may do this by sifting the ingredients together). Add the softened butter there is no butter visible and it's well incorporated into the dry.

3. Next, add milk and eggs in a jug and whisk until well combined.

4. Add wet ingredients to dry ingredients in a slow and steady stream until no dry ingredients are visible. Scrape down the bowl and mix for another 20 seconds.

5. Fill 6 donut tray cavities with chocolate batter at about the half way mark. Add the rest of the batter into a baking tray. Bake the donuts for 10 min and the rest of the batter for 20 min. Allow to cool completely.

6. Once the donuts and rest of cake have cooled, crumble the sheet cake into a large mixing bowl. Add frosting and mix well. Set aside.

7. Dip the donuts into the white chocolate coating them completely. Allow excess chocolate to drip off and place on a baking tray. Chill until set.

8. Add the coated donuts onto a cooling rack and portions of the blue and pink choc on

top. Gently tap the cooling rack to smoothen out the chocolate. Chill until set.

9. Dip each side of the top of the cones in the blue and pink chocolate as demonstrated. Allow to set before you fill with cake pop mixture.

10. Dip the tops of each filled cone into the white chocolate. And stick the donut on top of the cone. Allow to set.

11. Serve same day

Giant Donut

This is no mere cake made to look like a donut. Deep fried, this giant strawberry and raspberry jelly donut is the real deal.

Ingredients

Ganache

- 200g white cooking chocolate
- 100ml thickened/whipping cream
- 1tsp strawberries and cream essence (can sub for whatever essence flavour you like!)
- 2 drops pink food gel

Giant Donut

- 2 1/4 tsp active dry yeast
- 1/2 cup warm water, 110 degrees
- 1/4 cup granulated sugar
- 1/4 cup evaporated milk, warmed to 110 degrees
- 1/2 tsp salt

- 1/4 cup melted butter
- 1 large egg
- 1 egg yolk
- 1/2 tsp vanilla extract
- 420g 2 1/2 cups all-purpose flour, then more as needed
- 8 cups vegetable oil, for frying
- Funfetti sprinkles
- Cinnamon sugar to sprinkle
- 4 tbsp Raspberry Jam

Steps

Ganache

1. Add white chocolate and cream into a large microwave safe bowl. Microwave for 20

seconds at a time, mixing each time until smooth.

2. Add pink food gel and essence and mix until evenly coloured and well combined.
3. Alternatively you may melt it using a double boiler. Fill a medium sized pot with 1/3 of the way with water. Bring to a boil. Place bowl with chocolate and cream over the top and gently mix until mixture is completely melted and smooth.
4. To soften the ganache to spreading or piping consistency microwave for 10 seconds at a time, mixing each time with a large spatula until it reaches the right consistency.

Giant Donut

1. In a small bowl, whisk together yeast, warm water and 1/2 tsp of the sugar.
2. Cover it with cling wrap and a towel. Let it rest 5 - 10 minutes in a warm spot until it becomes frothy.
3. Add in yeast mixture, milk, remaining granulated sugar, salt, melted butter, egg, egg yolk and vanilla.
4. Add half of the flour and set mixer with whisk attachment and blend until smooth.
5. Switch mixer to hook attachment, slowly add remaining flour and knead on low

speed until smooth and elastic about 4 - 5 minutes, adding additional flour as needed (I only added about 2 Tbsp more. You shouldn't need a lot more, you want dough to be slightly sticky and tacky but shouldn't stick to a clean fingertip).

6. Transfer dough to a lightly oiled bowl, cover with plastic wrap and let rise in a warm place until double in size, about 1 1/2 hours.

7. Dust your work surface very well with flour. Gently tip your dough out of the bowl onto your work surface. Flatten slightly with the palm of your hands.

8. 10 minutes before the dough finishes rising gently heat up a large pot of oil.

9. Use a 7" cutter to cut the dough into a large circle shape. Use a 3" cookie cutter to cut the hole from the centre. When cutting the dough take care not to twist the cookie cutters while cutting the dough. Just very firmly cut in one motion until the dough cleanly comes away with your hand.

10. Carefully place a large pizza spatula under the large donut taking care not to misshape the dough. Take your time with this.

11. Using a kitchen spatula gently shuffle the dough off the pizza spatula into the oil.

Again, take your time with this making sure not to misshape the dough.

12. Fry on one side for 5 minutes until golden brown on a medium heat and finish off frying on the other side for a final 5 minutes. To flip the doughnut over make sure your pot of oil is at least 3cm wider than your donut on each side. Use two kitchen spatulas to flip. Put on in the hole and one underneath the donut and gently tip over as demonstrated. To take out of the oil use two flat spatulas and place underneath the donut on either side.

13. Place on a prepared baking tray lined with kitchen towels to let the oil drain.

14. Once the donut has cooled slightly, sprinkle with cinnamon sugar and use a serrated knife to cut in half. Again, I know I've said this a million times but take your time with this. The donut will be quite soft and fluffy.

15. Spread raspberry jam in the middle and sandwich backup again with the other half.

16. To finished off drizzle pink ganache over the top allowing some to drip off the sides and sprinkle with funfetti sprinkles.

17. Donuts are best served the day they're made.

Golden Doughnuts

You've literally struck gold with these mini doughnuts coated in glamorous edible gold leaf.

Ingredients

Doughnut Batter

- 1 cup all-purpose flour
- 1 tsp baking powder
- ¼ tsp salt
- 3 tbsp unsalted butter, melted
- ¼ cup sugar
- 2 tbsp honey
- 1 large egg
- 1 tsp vanilla extract

- 1/3 cup + 1 tbsp buttermilk
- 2 tbsp gold sprinkles

Glaze

- 3 tbsp whipping cream
- ½ cup confectioner's sugar
- yellow food colouring
- Edible gold leaf

Steps

Doughnut Batter

1. Whisk together the flour, baking powder and salt in a small bowl and set aside.
2. In a large bowl, combine the butter, sugar, honey, egg and vanilla extract.
3. Add the buttermilk and mix until combined.

4. Add the dry ingredients and sprinkles and mix until just combined – make sure not to over mix.
5. Spoon the batter into a piping bag.
6. Pipe the batter into a greased doughnut pan and bake at 400F for 7 minutes.
7. Cool for 1 minute in the pan, then flip the pan over to remove the doughnuts and cool completely on a wire rack.!

Glaze

1. Make the glaze: Whisk together the whipping cream and the confectioner's sugar and whisk until fully combined.

2. Dye the glaze a vibrant yellow colour. Dunk each doughnut into the glaze and return to the wire rack.

3. Cover the entire surface with edible gold leaf sheets, by gently applying with a clean, dry paintbrush. Do not use your fingers, because the gold leaf is sticky and will not transfer onto the doughnuts. Enjoy!

Homemade French Toast Balls

There's no denying that French toast is incredibly yummy, but it's even better in deep-fried, bite-sized form.

Ingredients

- 2 teaspoons dry active yeast

- 1 cup lukewarm water
- 1/2 cup + 1 teaspoon sugar
- 4 cups all-purpose flour
- 2 teaspoons salt
- 1 large egg yolk
- 2 large eggs
- 1/4 cup canola oil
- 1/2 cup cinnamon sugar
- 1/2 cup maple syrup

Steps

1. Mix warm water, yeast and a teaspoon of sugar. Let sit for 5 minutes.

2. Place remaining sugar, flour and salt in a stand mixer fitted with dough hook attachment.
3. Slowly pour in eggs, yolk and oil and mix until you get a shaggy dough. Pour in the yeast mixture.
4. Knead dough for 8 minutes and transfer to a well-oiled glass bowl. Cover with a damp tea towel and let rise for 1 to 2 hours until doubled in size.
5. Roll out the dough on a lightly floured surface into a 1/4 inch thick round. Cut into circles using a 2-inch biscuit cutter.

6. In a large Dutch oven filled with 4 inches of canola oil, fry the dough at 350 degrees or until golden on each side.

7. Place on paper towel to drain for one minute. Roll in cinnamon sugar and drizzle with maple syrup while still warm.

Gulab Jamun (Indian Doughnuts)

Soaked in sweet syrup, these Indian-style doughnuts can be enjoyed warm, hot or cold!

Ingredients

- 1 cup powdered milk
- 5 tablespoons all-purpose flour
- 1/4 teaspoon baking powder
- Pinch of salt

- 2 tablespoons butter, melted
- 3 tablespoons milk
- Ghee, to grease your hands
- 2 cups water
- 1 1/2 cup sugar
- 1/4 teaspoon rose essence (or 1 teaspoon rose water)
- A pinch of saffron
- Oil for frying (canola/begetable)

Steps

1. Combine powdered milk, flour, baking powder and salt.
2. Stir to combine.

3. Add melted butter and add milk, and gently stir until all ingredients are incorporated and form a thick dough.
4. Allow formed dough to sit at room temperature for 5 minutes to slightly firm up.
5. Prepare syrup by heating water and sugar, and simmer for 5 minutes until sugar has dissolved and slightly thickened.
6. Add rose essence and saffron.
7. Grease hands with ghee.
8. Gently form small balls with dough (approximately 1-1 1/2 inches in diameter), making sure not to overwork the dough.

(This can lead to a tough Gulab Jamun, so be careful.)

9. Heat 2-3 inches of oil in a deep pan on medium heat.

10. Add balls, and cook for 5-7 minutes until dark brown in color.

11. Immerse the hot Gulab Jamun balls immediately into the syrup, and allow to soak for a minimum of 10 minutes. The Gulab Jamun will puff up as they soak.

12. Serve warm, hot, cold - whichever way you like!

Chocolate-Filled Donut

With a crispy chocolate base, brigadeiro cream filling and sprinkles, this rich dessert is ridiculously chocolatey.

Ingredients

- 3 3/4 cups flour
- 1/2 cup cocoa powder
- 1 teaspoon baking powder
- 1/2 teaspoon baking soda
- 1/3 cup unsalted butter, room temperature
- 3/4 cup granulated sugar
- 1 egg
- 2/3 cup semi-sweet chocolate, melted
- 1 1/4 cups milk

- Oil, for deep-frying
- 1 cup brigadeiro chocolate truffle mixture
- 1 cup chocolate sprinkles

Steps

1. In a bowl, mix the flour, cocoa, baking powder and baking soda. Set aside.
2. Using a mixer, beat the butter with the sugar until it reaches a fluffy consistency. Add the egg, and continue to mix until combined. Use a spatula to fold in melted chocolate.
3. Stir in half of the dry ingredients, then add the milk, continuing to stir to combine. Mix

in the rest of the dry ingredients, stirring with a wooden spoon.

4. Spread the mixture onto a baking pan covered in wax paper and refrigerate for 30 minutes.
5. Use a round cookie cutter (about 3 inches in diameter) to cut circles out of the dough. Use a smaller cutter (about 1 inch in diameter) to punch a hole in the center of each circle, forming donuts.
6. Deep-fry in hot oil and drain on paper towels.
7. Using a toothpick, make small holes in the top of the donuts. Transfer brigadeiro

mixture to a pastry sleeve and fill the donuts with the mixture.

8. Decorate with Brigadeiro mixture and chocolate sprinkles.

Giant Glazed Donut Cake

This humongous glazed cake topped with colorful sprinkles will appeal to donut and cake lovers alike.

Ingredients

- 185 grams Unsalted Butter
- 200 grams Caster Sugar
- 3 Eggs
- 200 grams Plain Flour
- Pinch Salt

- 1 1/4 teaspoon Baking Powder
- 165 milliliters Milk
- 1 teaspoon Vanilla Extract
- Glaze
- 95 grams Icing Sugar
- 1 tablespoon Butter, Melted
- 1-2 tablespoons Milk
- 1/2 teaspoon Vanilla Extract
- Pink Food Coloring
- Sprinkles

Steps

1. Melt the butter in a pan, stirring constantly until the butter has turned brown and

taken on a nutty smell (10-12m). Pour this into a bowl and allow to cool to room temperature.
2. Once cooled, add the butter, sugar and salt to a stand mixer and beat for 5m until light and fluffy.
3. Add the eggs one at a time on high speed until incorporated.
4. Mix the flour and baking powder together, add it to the butter mixture in 3 parts, alternating with the milk & vanilla in 2 parts.
5. Add to a silicone mould or bundt tin and bake at 180C/375F for 40-45m. Allow to cool completely.

6. To make the glaze, add the icing sugar, melted butter, vanilla and pink food colouring to a bowl. Slowly add the milk until you have a thick glaze consistency.

7. Pour the glaze over the cooled cake and top with sprinkles.

Rainbow-Filled Doughnuts

If you like vanilla cream-stuffed doughnuts, you'll love this colorful twist on a favorite.

Ingredients

Doughnuts

- 2 tablespoons active dry yeast
- 1/2 cup warm water

- 1 teaspoon granulated sugar
- 2 1/2 cups all-purpose flour
- 1/4 cup granulated sugar
- 2 large eggs
- 2 tablespoons unsalted butter, room temperature
- 2 teaspoons salt
- Canola oil

Glaze

- 1 1/2 cups confectioner's sugar
- 1/2 cup whipping cream
- Rainbow sprinkles

Rainbow Filling

- 2 1/2 cups vanilla pudding

- Rainbow food colouring

Steps

Doughnuts

1. Make the doughnuts: Place the yeast, warm water and 1 teaspoon granulated sugar into the bowl of an electric mixer fitted with the dough hook attachment.
2. Allow this to sit for 10 minutes, until the yeast begins to develop.
3. Add the flour, 1/2 cup sugar, eggs, butter and salt. Set the mixer to medium speed and knead for 8-9 minutes, until the dough is smooth, soft and bounces back when poked with your finger.

4. Place the dough in an oiled bowl and cover with plastic wrap.
5. Place in a warm spot until doubled in size, about 1 hour.
6. Roll the dough out to 1/4 inch-thick and cut into 2 1/2 inch-wide circles with a cookie cutter. You should be able to get 15-20 doughnuts. Transfer the doughnuts to a lightly floured baking sheet and cover with a sheet of plastic wrap.
7. Place in a warm spot and let rise for 20 minutes.
8. Pour about 5 inches of canola oil into a pot and set to medium heat.

9. Attach a deep-fry thermometer and heat the oil to 370F.
10. Fry 3 or 4 doughnuts at a time, cooking for 1 minute on each side or until golden.
11. Remove the doughnuts from the oil with a slotted spoon and place on a baking sheet lined with paper towel.
12. Cool completely.

Glaze

1. Make the glaze: Combine the confectioner's sugar and whipping cream in a bowl.
2. Set aside.

Rainbow Filling

1. Make the filling: Divide the pudding into 6 bowls and dye them the colours of the rainbow.
2. Place the pudding into piping bags fitted with round piping tips.
3. Assembly: Poke holes in each doughnut with the end of a fork.
4. Squirt a dollop of each colour of pudding into each doughnut in the colour of the rainbow.
5. Dunk the doughnuts into the glaze, then sprinkle with rainbow sprinkles. Enjoy!

Avoca-Donuts

The perfect sweet treat for avocado lovers who may be tired of plain old avocado toast.

Ingredients

- **Donuts:**

    - 1 1/2 cups flour
    - 1/3 cup cocoa powder
    - 1 teaspoon baking soda
    - 1/2 teaspoon salt
    - 1 ripe avocado, mashed
    - 1 cup milk
    - 3/4 cup maple syrup
    - 2 teaspoons vanilla
    - 1 teaspoon apple cider vinegar

- **Frosting:**

    - 1 ripe avocado
    - 1 tablespoon butter, softened
    - 1/2 teaspoon vanilla extract
    - Pinch salt
    - 2 cups powdered sugar
    - Chocolate sprinkles

Steps

1. Preheat oven to 350°F. Grease donut pan with baking spray.
2. Mix dry donut ingredients in a bowl and set aside.

3. In a separate bowl, mix wet ingredients until combined, making sure there are no avocado lumps. Add wet to dry, and mix.
4. Pour into donut pan and bake for about 22 minutes.
5. Make the frosting. Using a mixer, beat avocado and butter until combined and no lumps remain. Beat in vanilla and salt. Add powdered sugar slowly and mix until combined, adding more until desired consistency.
6. Once donuts are done, remove from oven and let cool. Top with frosting and chocolate sprinkles!

Smores Freakshake Cupcakes

It's everything you love about s'mores packed into a cupcake and topped with a mini doughnut.

Ingredients

Smore's Freakshake Cupcakes

- 50 grams cocoa powder
- 175 grams all-purpose flour
- 1/2 teaspoon salt
- 1/2 teaspoon bicarbonate of soda
- 225 grams caster sugar
- 175 grams unsalted butter, softened
- 2 large eggs, at room temperature
- 1 teaspoon vanilla extract
- 175 milliliters milk

- 12 marshmallows
- Crushed and chopped graham crackers
- Chocolate sauce
- 250 grams marshmallow fluff

Donuts

- 2 1/4 teaspoon active dry yeast
- 1/2 cup warm water, 110 degrees
- 1/4 cup granulated sugar
- 1/4 cup evaporated milk, warmed to 110 degrees
- 1/2 teaspoon salt
- 1/4 cup melted butter
- 1 large egg
- 1 egg yolk

- 1/2 teaspoon vanilla extract
- 420 grams 2 1/2 cups all-purpose flour, then more as needed
- Cinnamon sugar
- 3 - 4 cups vegetable oil, for frying

Frosting

- 1 batch fluffy chocolate ganache frosting

Steps

Smore's Freakshake Cupcakes

1. Preheat a fan-forced oven to 160C (320F) or 180C (356F) for a conventional oven.
2. Line a cupcake tin with cupcake liners.

3. In the bowl of a stand mixer fitted with the paddle attachment, add the cocoa powder, plain flour, salt, bicarb soda and sugar. Turn mixer on low speed and allow it to mix for a couple minutes to help everything combine well!(alternatively you may do this by sifting the ingredients together).
4. Add the softened butter there is no butter visible and it's well incorporated into the dry.
5. Next, add milk and eggs in a jug and whisk until well combined.
6. Add wet ingredients to dry ingredients in a slow and steady stream until no dry

ingredients are visible. Scrape down the bowl and mix for another 20 seconds.

7. Fill each paper 3/4 of the way (using an ice cream scoop to transfer the batter into the cupcake liners makes this a quick and easy process otherwise you can use two tablespoons).
8. Sprinkle crushed graham crackers on top.
9. Bake for 20-25 min or until a toothpick inserted comes out clean.
10. Allow them to cool completely on a wire cooling rack before frosting.
11. Core the centre of each cupcake and fill with marshmallow fluff.

12. Fit the end of a piping bag with a large round tip and frost a double donut swirl on top.

13. Drizzle chocolate sauce.

14. Place donut on top. I cut off a little of the bottom of the donut to help it sit on the frosting a little better.

15. Drizzle chocolate sauce on the donut.

16. Place marshmallow and graham cracker on top. Toast marshmallow using a kitchen torch. Alternatively you can pre toast it by placing it on a metal skewer and placing it over a gas stove top. Make sure you don't burn the house to cinders.

Donuts

1. (Please note, you'll probs want to make the donut while the cupcakes are baking)
2. In a small bowl, whisk together yeast, warm water and 1/2 teaspoon of the sugar.
3. Cover it with cling wrap and a towel. Let it rest 5 - 10 minutes in a warm spot until it becomes frothy.
4. Add in yeast mixture, milk, remaining granulated sugar, salt, melted butter, egg, egg yolk and vanilla.
5. Add half of the flour and set mixer with whisk attachment and blend until smooth. Switch mixer to hook attachment, slowly add remaining flour and knead on low speed until smooth and elastic about 4 - 5

minutes, adding additional flour as needed (I only added about 2 tablespoons more. You shouldn't need a lot more, you want dough to be slightly sticky and tacky but shouldn't stick to a clean fingertip). Transfer dough to a lightly oiled bowl, cover with plastic wrap and let rise in a warm place until double in size, about 1 1/2 hours.

6. Roll dough into an even layer onto a floured surface to slightly less than 1/2-inch thickness.

7. Cut into doughnut shapes using a 2 inch cookie cutter. Use a smaller cookie cutter or the end of a piping tip to cut out little

donut holes. Cover with a clean tea towel and let them rise in a warm spot until doubled, about 30 - 40 minutes.

8. Preheat the oil in a large pot on medium high heat. Drop a small amount of dough into the oil and if it bubbles and fizzes around the sides the oil is hot enough. Gently and carefully drop donuts into the oil. Don't add more than three donuts at a time. Cook them on one side until they're a light golden brown then flip them over.

9. Once they're golden on both sides carefully take them out and transfer them to a plate lined with kitchen paper towels to let the oil drain.

10. To finish off the donuts roll them around in some cinnamon sugar.

11. Donuts are best served the day they're made.

Boston Cream Donuts

Filled with vanilla custard and dipped in chocolate, these doughnuts would make Boston proud.

Ingredients

Chocolate Glaze

- 1 cup powdered sugar
- 1/4 cup unsweetened cocoa powder
- 1/4 cup milk

- 1 teaspoon vanilla extract

Pastry Cream

- 1 (3.4 ounces) package instant vanilla pudding
- 1 cup whole milk, cold
- 1 cup heavy cream, cold
- 1 teaspoon vanilla extract

Donuts

- 2 package puff pastries, thawed
- 1 egg, lightly beaten
- Canola oil for frying

Steps

Chocolate Glaze

1. In a medium bowl, whisk together the powdered sugar, unsweetened cocoa powder, milk and vanilla until smooth. Set aside.

Pastry Cream

1. In a medium bowl, add pudding mix and milk, and whisk until combined.
2. Pour in heavy cream and whisk until fully incorporated.
3. Add vanilla extract and whisk again until pudding has thickened.
4. Let it sit for 5 minutes.

5. Fill a pastry bag fitted with a large round tip.

Donuts

1. Fill a large Dutch oven halfway with canola oil.
2. Heat oil to 365°F.
3. Dust a cutting board with flour.
4. Unfold both puff pastries and open flat.
5. Brush 1 pastry with egg wash. Top with other puff pastry.
6. With a 3-inch round cookie cutter, cut out 9 rounds.
7. Lay on sheet tray. Gently push down around the edges of each round. Pierce

each round in the middle with a toothpick three times.

8. Place in freezer for 10 minutes.

9. Remove from freezer, and transfer puff pastry rounds to the hot oil.

10. Fry for 5 minutes, then flip to cook the other side for 2-3 minutes, or until a deep golden brown.

11. Drain on a paper towel. Let sit for 3 minutes until cool enough to pick up.

12. To fill the doughnuts with cream, insert the tip of the pastry bag filled with cream into the side of the doughnut and squeeze.

13. Gently dip one side into the chocolate glaze. Place on rack to let dry. Serve.

Chocolate Samoa Cake Donuts

One of your favorite Girl Scout Cookies is now in fluffy, chocolatey donut form.

Ingredients

- 50 grams cocoa powder
- 175 grams all-purpose flour
- 1/2 teaspoon salt
- 1/2 teaspoon bicarbonate of soda
- 225 grams caster sugar
- 175 grams unsalted butter, softened
- 2 large eggs, at room temperature

- 1 teaspoon vanilla extract
- 175 milliliters milk
- 200 grams melted chocolate
- Samoa Mixture
- 250 ounce bag of caramel, unwrap all of the caramels, set aside
- 1 cup shredded unsweetened coconut, toasted
- 5 tablespoons milk
- 1/4 teaspoon salt

Steps

1. Samoa Mixture
2. Melt unwrapped caramels and milk in a medium mixing bowl for 1 minutes, remove

from microwave and stir, then place back in microwave for 30 seconds and stir again. Repeat process until caramel is completely melted and smooth, stir in salt and toasted coconut.

3. Cupcakes

4. Preheat a fan-forced oven to 180C (356F) or 160C (320F) for a fan forced oven. Use vegetable oil spray / cooking spray to oil a cake donut baking tray.

5. In the bowl of a stand mixer fitted with the paddle attachment, add the cocoa powder, plain flour, salt, bicarb soda and sugar. Turn mixer on low speed and allow it to mix for a couple minutes to help everything

combine well! (alternatively you may do this by sifting the ingredients together). Add the softened butter there is no butter visible and it's well incorporated into the dry.

6. Next, add milk and eggs in a jug and whisk until well combined.

7. Add wet ingredients to dry ingredients in a slow and steady stream until no dry ingredients are visible. Scrape down the bowl and mix for another 20 seconds.

8. Transfer batter to a piping bag or zip lock bag and pipe batter into donut tray filling up half way. Bake for 12 min or until a skewer inserted into the cake comes out

clean. Gently tap the tray onto a clean bench to help the donuts come out. Transfer to a cooling rack.

9. Add a tablespoon of Samoa mixture and sandwich with another cake donut.

10.   Finish off with a drizzle of melted chocolate.

Apple Pie Donuts

Pillowy cinnamon donuts are topped with glaze, crushed shortbread cookies and sweet apples.

Ingredients

- **Doughnuts**

  - 2 1/4 teaspoon active dry yeast
  - 1/2 cup warm water, 110 degrees

- 1/4 cup granulated sugar
- 1/4 cup evaporated milk, warmed to 110 degrees
- 1/4 cup melted butter
- 1 large egg
- 1 egg yolk
- 2 1/2 cups all-purpose flour, then more as needed
- 3 - 4 cups vegetable oil , for frying
- Crushed butter cookies
- 3 green apples
- 1 tablespoon lemon juice
- 1/4 cup granulated sugar
- 1 teaspoon powdered cinnamon
- 1 cup powdered sugar

- 2 tablespoons milk
- 1 teaspoon cinnamon

Steps

1. To make the glaze, combine sugar and cinnamon, add milk and mix until well combined. Cover with plastic wrap and set aside.
2. To make the apple pie, peel, core and dice apples. Add to a medium sized saucepan along with lemon juice, sugar and cinnamon. Continue cooking until tender and a syrup sauce develops. Cover and set aside to cool.

3. In the bowl of an electric stand mixer, whisk together yeast, warm water and 1/2 teaspoon of the sugar.
4. Cover it with cling wrap and a towel. Let it rest 5 - 10 minutes in a warm spot until it becomes frothy.
5. Add in milk, remaining granulated sugar, cinnamon, melted butter, egg and egg yolk.
6. Add half of the flour and set mixer with whisk attachment and blend until smooth. Switch mixer to hook attachment, slowly add remaining flour and knead on low speed until smooth and elastic about 4 - 5 minutes, adding additional flour as needed

(I only added about 2 tablespoons more. You shouldn't need a lot more, you want dough to be slightly sticky and tacky but shouldn't stick to a clean fingertip).

7. Transfer dough to a lightly oiled bowl, cover with plastic wrap and let rise in a warm place until double in size, about 1 1/2 hours.

8. Punch dough down and roll into an even layer onto a floured surface to slightly less than 1/2-inch thickness. Cut into doughnut shapes using a 3 inch cookie cutter. Cover with a clean tea towel and let them rise in a warm spot until doubled, about 30 - 40 minutes.

9. Preheat the oil in a large pot on medium high heat. Drop a small amount of dough into the oil and if it bubbles and fizzes around the sides the oil is hot enough.
10. Gently and carefully drop donuts into the oil. Don't add more than three donuts at a time. Cook them on one side until they're a light golden brown then flip them over. Once they're golden on both sides carefully take them out and transfer them to a plate lined with kitchen paper towels to let the oil drain.
11. Roll around in cinnamon sugar. To finish, drizzle with glaze, sprinkle crushed cookies and add a heap of apple pie mix.

12. Donuts are best served the day they're made.

Easy Croissant Donuts

Yummy, chocolate-dipped cronuts are simpler to make than you might think.

Ingredients

- 2 sheets puff pastry
- 200 grams pancake mix
- 1 egg
- 20 grams butter
- 30 grams sugar
- Chocolate, melted

• Toppings:

- Crushed pistachio

- Pink peppercorns
- Gold leaf
- Dried fruits
- Freeze-dried raspberries

Steps

1. Soften puff pastry and butter at room temperature.
2. In a bowl, combine pancake mix, egg, butter and sugar and mix well.
3. Roll out and flatten dough with a pastry roller. Place puff pastry on top.
4. Wrap the dough around the puff pastry. Cut in half and roll out to flatten. Repeat this process three times.

5. Using a mold, cut out donuts.

6. Fry in hot oil (170 degrees C) until golden brown.

7. Dip in melted chocolate and decorate with your favorite toppings.

Birthday Cake Baked Donuts

For your next party, skip a basic cake and embrace yummy donuts instead.

Ingredients

Donuts

- 1 cup all-purpose flour
- 1 teaspoon baking powder
- 1/4 teaspoon baking soda
- 1/3 cup granulated sugar

- 1/4 cup greek yogurt
- 1/4 cup whole milk
- 1 large egg
- 2 tablespoons unsalted butter, melted
- 1 teaspoon vanilla extract
- 1/3 cup rainbow sprinkles

Glaze

- 3/4 cup powdered sugar
- 1 1/2 tablespoon unsalted butter
- 1 teaspoon vanilla extract
- 1 pinch salt
- 1-2 tablespoons milk
- Rainbow sprinkles

Steps

Donuts

1. Preheat oven to 350°F.
2. In a bowl, whisk the flour, baking powder, baking soda, and sugar together.
3. In another bowl, combine milk, yogurt, egg, melted butter, and vanilla.
4. Pour the wet ingredients into the dry, and stir well.
5. Using a spatula, gently fold the sprinkles into the batter.
6. Use a piping bag to fill each well of a greased 6-cup donut pan. Fill about 3/4 of the way.

7. Bake for about 8-10 minutes or until the lightly browned and when a toothpick comes out clean when inserted.
8. Remove from oven and transfer to a rack to cool.

Glaze

1. Meanwhile, in a bowl, whisk together powdered sugar, melted butter, vanilla extract, salt, and 1 tablespoon of milk.
2. Add some additional milk, if the consistency is too thick.
3. Heat in the microwave until slightly warmed.

4. Once the donuts have cooled, dip in the warm glaze and set aside on the rack.

5. Immediately top with sprinkles and allow the glaze to set.

Dukkah Donuts With Blood Orange Glaze

Vanilla donuts with a citrus glaze and nutty topping will be the highlight of your brunch.

Ingredients

Donuts

- 1 3/4 cups flour
- 1 cup sugar
- 1 teaspoon baking powder
- 1/2 teaspoon baking soda
- 3/4 teaspoon kosher salt

- 1 large egg
- 1/2 cup buttermilk
- 1/4 cup flavorless oil
- 1 teaspoon vanilla extract
- 1/4 cup water

Blood Orange Glaze

- 3 cups powdered sugar
- 2 tablespoons honey
- 4 to 5 tablespoons fresh blood orange juice (about 2 blood oranges)

Dukkah

- 1/4 cup hazelnuts, toasted and coarsely ground
- 1/4 cup toasted sesame seeds

- 1 tablespoon ground anise seeds
- 1 tablespoon coriander seeds, toasted and coarsely ground
- A pinch of kosher salt

Steps

Donuts

1. Preheat oven to 375°F.
2. Coat a 12-cavity donut pan with cooking spray.
3. In a large bowl, whisk together flour, sugar, baking powder, baking soda and salt.
4. In a medium bowl, whisk together the egg, buttermilk, oil, vanilla and water. Whisk the

wet mixture into the dry mixture and stir to combine.

5. Fill a piping bag (with no tip) with the batter and pipe the batter into the donut cavities, filling each halfway. This could get a little messy.

6. Bake until a toothpick inserted into a donut comes out clean, about 12 minutes.

7. Cool in the pan for 5 minutes, then remove to a wire rack to cool completely.

Blood Orange Glaze

1. To make the glaze: In a small bowl, mix together the powdered sugar, honey and 4 tablespoons orange juice. Add more juice

little by little until the mixture is spreadable (you might not need the full remaining tablespoon). It should be quite thick yet spreadable.

Dukkah

1. Combine all ingredients for the dukkah in a small bowl and mix.
2. Dip the donuts halfway into the glaze, then allow excess glaze to drip off.
3. Sprinkle the tops with dukkah and enjoy.

Sun-Dried Tomato Basil Doughnuts With Cheese Filling

These cheese-stuffed bites are the socially acceptable way to eat doughnuts for dinner.

Ingredients

- 1 1/8 teaspoon dry-active yeast
- 1/2 cup whole milk, warmed to 110°F
- 2 tablespoons unsalted butter, softened
- 2 teaspoons sugar
- 1 1/3 cups flour
- 1/2 teaspoon salt
- 1 egg
- 2 tablespoons fresh basil, finely chopped
- 1 teaspoon fresh oregano, finely chopped
- 1/4 cup sun-dried tomatoes (not packed in oil), finely chopped
- 1/4 cup shredded mozzarella

- 6 ounces block cheddar cheese, cut into 15 cubes (or as many doughnuts as you made)
- 1 bottle canola oil (about 40 fl. oz.), for frying

Steps

1. In a small bowl, mix together the warm milk and yeast. Let sit for 5 minutes until frothy.
2. In a stand mixer fitted with a dough hook, mix together the butter, sugar, flour, salt and egg. Next, add in the activated yeast and milk. Put the machine on medium and beat with the dough hook for 5 minutes

until a nice dough has formed. Lastly, add the basil, oregano, sun-dried tomatoes, and mozzarella. Mix until incorporated.

3. Cover the bowl with a clean kitchen towel and let rise in a warm place for 1-2 hours.

4. Once risen, remove the dough from the bowl and roll into a 10-inch rectangle. Cut out 2-inch circles. Re-roll the dough, keeping the same 1 1/2-inch thickness until all the dough is used up and you've created about 15 rounds.

5. Place one cube of cheese in the center of each round and pinch to close the dough over the the cheese, being sure to completely seal the cheese inside. Roll the

dough back into a round disc shape and continue with remaining dough. Once all the rounds have been filled, place on parchment paper and cover with a clean kitchen towel for an additional 20 minutes until puffed up again.

6. Meanwhile, heat your oil. Place oil in a medium pot and attach a candy thermometer to the side. Heat oil until it reaches 325°F.

7. Put 3-4 doughnuts in the oil at a time, frying for about 3 minutes on the first side, and 2-3 minutes on the other. Keep checking to ensure your oil remains at

325°F and that your doughnuts are deeply golden brown.

8. Remove doughnuts with a slotted spoon to a plate lined with paper towels. Continue with remaining rounds.

9. Serve fresh from the oil as they are best hot!

Monster Donuts

Because everyone knows breakfast treats that can bite back are just better.

Ingredients

Monster Donuts

- 215 grams flour
- 1 1/2 teaspoon baking powder

- 132 grams sugar
- 187 milliliters milk
- 65 milliliters oil
- 60 grams butter
- 1 tablespoon yogurt
- 1 egg
- 1/2 teaspoon vanilla extract
- Purple food dye

Monster Eyes

- 100 grams melted white choc
- Green sprinkles (for eyes)
- Chocolate Monster Hair
- 200 grams white chocolate

- 80 milliliters cream (at least 35 percent fat content)
- 2 drops green food dye
- 1 drop yellow food dye

Steps

Monster Donuts

1. Preheat a fan-forced oven to 180C (356F) or 160C (320F) for a fan-forced oven. Spray a donut baking tray with cooking oil and set aside.
2. In the bowl of a stand mixer fitted with the paddle attachment, add the flour, baking

powder, caster sugar and salt. Turn the mixer on low speed and allow it to mix for a couple of minutes to help everything combine well (alternatively you may do this by sifting the ingredients together). Add the softened butter and let it mix until it resembles a fine sand-like texture.

3. Next, add milk, eggs, yogurt, oil and vanilla extract in a large jug and whisk well.

4. Add wet ingredients to dry ingredients in a slow and steady stream until no dry ingredients are visible. Scrape down the bowl and mix for another 20 seconds.

5. Fill donut tray holes 1/2 way and bake for 12 min. Once baked transfer to a cooking wrack to cool down completely.

6. Add green ganache to a piping or zip lock bag and pipe little spikes on the top of each donut.

7. Finish off by randomly placing monster eyes on ganache before serving.

Monster Eyes

1. To make monster eyes, add melted white choc to a piping or sip lock bag and pipe little dollops of choc on a sheet of baking paper. Place a green sprinkle on each one before it sets.

Chocolate Monster Hair

1. To prepare Chocolate Monster Hair add cream and chocolate to a microwave safe bowl and microwave for 20 seconds at a time, mixing each time until smooth.

2. Add green and yellow food dye and mix until well combined. Chill for 1 hour and allow to set.

Maple Syrup Doughnuts

You'll totally fall for these adorably delicious donuts.

Ingredients

Doughnut Batter

- 3 tablespoons unsalted butter, melted

- 1 cup all-purpose flour
- 1 teaspoon baking powder
- 1/4 teaspoon salt
- 1/4 cup granulated sugar
- 2 tablespoons maple syrup
- 1 large egg
- 1/2 teaspoon vanilla extract
- 1/3 cup + 1 tablespoon buttermilk
- Maple syrup

Glaze

- 2 tablespoons maple syrup
- 2 tablespoons whipping cream
- 1/2 cup confectioner's sugar
- Brown food colouring

- Maple leaf candies, for decoration

Steps

Doughnut Batter

1. Whisk together the flour, baking powder and salt in a small bowl and set aside.
2. In a large bowl, combine the butter, sugar, maple syrup, egg and vanilla extract.
3. Add the buttermilk and mix until combined.
4. Add the dry ingredients and mix until just combined - make sure not to over mix.
5. Place the batter in a piping bag fitted with a round piping tip.
6. Pipe the batter into a greased doughnut pan and bake at 400F for 7 minutes.

7. Cool for 1 minute in the pan, then flip the pan over to remove the doughnuts and brush some maple syrup on top.
8. Cool completely on a wire rack.

Glaze

1. Make the glaze: Whisk together the maple syrup, whipping cream and confectioner's sugar until fully combined. If desired, add some brown food colouring and mix to combine.
2. Dunk each doughnut into the glaze and return to the wire rack.
3. Top with maple leaf candies and enjoy!

Chocolate Strawberry Cheesecake Donuts

When you crave dessert for breakfast, look no further than this chocolatey cheesecake doughnut.

Ingredients

Choc Strawberry Cheesecake Donuts (Makes 12)

- Doughnuts
- 2 1/4 teaspoon active dry yeast
- 1/2 cup warm water, 110 degrees
- 1/4 cup granulated sugar

- 1/4 cup evaporated milk, warmed to 110 degrees
- 1/2 teaspoon salt
- 1/4 cup melted butter
- 1 large egg
- 1 egg yolk
- 1/2 teaspoon vanilla extract
- 2 1/2 cups all-purpose flour, then more as needed
- 3 - 4 cups vegetable shortening, for frying
- Chocolate sauce
- Fresh strawberries
- Crushed shortbread cookies

Cheesecake Filling

- 400 grams Philadelphia cream cheese
- 200 milliliters sweetened condensed milk
- 1 teaspoon vanilla bean paste

Steps

Choc Strawberry Cheesecake Donuts (Makes 12)

1. In the bowl of an electric stand mixer, whisk together yeast, warm water and 1/2 teaspoon of the sugar. Cover it with cling wrap and a towel. Let it rest 5 - 10 minutes in a warm spot until it becomes frothy.

2. Add in milk, remaining granulated sugar (3 tablespoons + 2 1/2 teaspoon), salt, 1/4 cup shortening, egg, egg yolk and vanilla.
3. Add half of the flour and set mixer with whisk attachment and blend until smooth. Switch mixer to hook attachment, slowly add remaining flour and knead on low speed until smooth and elastic about 4 - 5 minutes, adding additional flour as needed (I only added about 2 tablespoons more. You shouldn't need a lot more, you want dough to be slightly sticky and tacky but shouldn't stick to a clean fingertip).
4. Transfer dough to a lightly oiled bowl, cover with plastic wrap and let rise in a

warm place until double in size, about 1 1/2 hours.

5. Punch dough down and roll into an even layer onto a floured surface to slightly less than 1/2-inch thickness. Cut into doughnut shapes using a 3 inch cookie cutter. Cover with a clean tea towel and let them rise in a warm spot until doubled, about 30 - 40 minutes.

6. Preheat the oil in a large pot on medium high heat. Drop a small amount of dough into the oil and if it bubbles and fizzes around the sides the oil is hot enough. Gently and carefully drop donuts into the

oil. Don't add more than three donuts at a time.

7. Cook them on one side until they're a light golden brown then flip them over. Once they're golden on both sides carefully take them out and transfer them to a plate lined with kitchen paper towels to let the oil drain.

8. While the donuts are cooling prepare the cheesecake filling by adding the cream cheese and sugar or sweetened condensed milk to a large mixing bowl. Use a wooden spoon to combine them or a hand mixer until the mixture is smooth. Transfer to a zip lock bag or piping bag.

9. To finish off the donuts simply poke a hole in the top of the donut and insert the bag with cheesecake filling in the donut. Fill with filling

10. Once all the donuts are filled drizzle with choc sauce, sprinkle with crushed shortbread cookies and place two halves of a strawberry on top. Donuts are best served the day they're made.

Cheesecake Filling

1. To make cheesecake filling add cream cheese to a large mixing bowl and mix with

a hand mixer to soften. Add sweetened condensed milk and vanilla bean paste.

Apple Doughnuts

Can a doughnut a day keep the doctor away? Just maybe.

Ingredients

- 2 medium apples, peeled
- 2 cups semisweet chocolate, broken into pieces
- 1/2 cup peanut butter
- Sprinkles for topping

Steps

1. Line a baking sheet with parchment paper.

2. Cut each apple into 4 or 5 even slices, about 1/2-inch thick. Using an apple corer, core each slice individually, making a perfect circle in the center of the apple slices.

3. Dry each slice off as much as possible using a paper towel.

4. Melt chocolate in a double boiler or in 30-second intervals in the microwave until completely melted.

5. Spread a layer of peanut butter (about 2 tablespoons) on the top of each apple.

6. Carefully dip each peanut-butter-topped apple slice in the chocolate to coat completely.

7. Drain off excess, then place on parchment paper. Continue with remaining apples.

8. Top each apple doughnut with sprinkles and refrigerate until firm, about 15 minutes. Eat immediately.

Nutella Cronuts

Deep-fried to golden perfection and stuffed with Nutella — what more could you want in a cronut?

Ingredients

- 1 block of pre-made puff pastry (320 grams or less)
- 5/6 tablespoon Nutella (or as much as your heart desires)
- As much chocolate sprinkles as you want

- 5 tablespoons of water
- Oil

Steps

1. Unroll the puff pastry and cut circles with a biscuit cutter.
2. Wet the first pastry disc, and add another on top. Do this until you have 4 discs stacked atop one another. Using a smaller biscuit cutter, cut another hole in the middle of those circles to create your fauxnut shape.
3. Deep fry the discs in a neutral oil at 180C. They'll be golden and puffed up when ready.

4. Drain the fauxnuts on kitchen paper. Once cooled, use a piping bag to pump Nutella into the fauxnuts.

5. Garnish with more Nutella and chocolate sprinkles.

Lemon Meringue Donuts

Stuffed with lemon curd and topped with meringue, some donuts go way beyond breakfast.

Ingredients

Lemon Meringue Donuts

- 2 1/4 teaspoon active dry yeast
- 1/2 cup warm water, 110 degrees
- 1/4 cup granulated sugar

- 1/4 cup evaporated milk, warmed to 110 degrees
- 1/2 teaspoon salt
- 1/4 cup melted butter
- 1 large egg
- 1 egg yolk
- 1/2 teaspoon vanilla extract
- 2 1/2 cups all-purpose flour, then more as needed
- 3 - 4 cups vegetable shortening, for frying
- 1 cup lemon curd
- Mint leaves to decorate

Meringue Frosting

- 4 egg whites (room temperature)
- 1 cups caster sugar
- 1 teaspoon vanilla extract

Steps

Lemon Meringue Donuts

1. In the bowl of an electric stand mixer, whisk together yeast, warm water and 1/2 teaspoon of the sugar. Cover it with cling wrap and a towel. Let it rest 5 - 10 minutes in a warm spot until it becomes frothy.
2. Add in milk, remaining granulated sugar (3 tablespoons + 2 1/2 teaspoon), salt, 1/4 cup shortening, egg, egg yolk and vanilla.

3. Add half of the flour and set mixer with whisk attachment and blend until smooth. Switch mixer to hook attachment, slowly add remaining flour and knead on low speed until smooth and elastic about 4 - 5 minutes, adding additional flour as needed (I only added about 2 tablespoons more. You shouldn't need a lot more, you want dough to be slightly sticky and tacky but shouldn't stick to a clean fingertip).
4. Transfer dough to a lightly oiled bowl, cover with plastic wrap and let rise in a warm place until double in size, about 1 1/2 hours.

5. Punch dough down and roll into an even layer onto a floured surface to slightly less than 1/2-inch thickness.
6. Cut into doughnut shapes using a 3 inch cookie cutter. Cover with a clean tea towel and let them rise in a warm spot until doubled, about 30 - 40 minutes.
7. Preheat the oil in a large pot on medium-high heat. Drop a small amount of dough into the oil and if it bubbles and fizzes around the sides the oil is hot enough.
8. Gently and carefully drop donuts into the oil. Don't add more than three donuts at a time. Cook them on one side until they're a light golden brown then flip them over.

Once they're golden on both sides carefully take them out and transfer them to a plate lined with kitchen paper towels to let the oil drain.

9. Add lemon curd to a piping or zip lock bag.
10. To finish off the donuts simply poke a hole in the top of the donut and insert the bag with lemon curd filling in the donut. Fill with filling. Once all the donuts are filled carefully roll the donuts around in cinnamon sugar.
11. Fit the end of a piping bag with an open star tip and frost as demonstrated in the video.

12. Finish off by toasting the meringue and garnish with mint leaves.

Meringue Frosting

1. Place about an inch of water to a medium-sized pot and bring it to the boil.
2. Add your egg whites, sugar and cream of tartar to a large, clean metal bowl. Mix using a whisk or handheld mixer to help combine all the ingredients.
3. Place the bowl with the egg mixture on top of your pot of boiling water making sure the bottom of the mixing bowl doesn't touch the bottom of the pot. Mix on high speed for 5 min or until the sugar in the

mixture completely dissolves. You can check this by dipping two (clean) fingers into the mixture and if you can't feel any grains of sugar it's ready to take off the pot. Mix on high speed once you've taken it off the heat (about 5-6 min) until the mixture cools down and gets thick and glossy. You want to reach stiff peaks so that the frosting holds its shape well.

Cinnamon Bun Doughnuts

We combined your two favorite morning indulgences into one.

Ingredients

Cinnamon Bun Doughnuts

- 3 tablespoons unsalted butter, melted
- 1 cup all-purpose flour
- 1 teaspoon baking powder
- 1/4 teaspoon salt
- 1/4 cup granulated sugar
- 2 tablespoons honey
- 1 large egg
- 1/2 teaspoon vanilla extract
- 1 teaspoon ground cinnamon
- 1/3 cup + 1 tablespoon buttermilk
- 1 teaspoon ground cinnamon
- 3 tablespoons brown sugar
- 2 tablespoons crushed pecans

Glaze

- 56 grams cream cheese, room temperature
- 1/3 cup confectioner's sugar
- 1 tablespoon milk

Steps

Cinnamon Bun Doughnuts

1. Whisk together the flour, baking powder, salt and cinnamon in a small bowl and set aside.
2. In a large bowl, combine the butter, sugar, honey and vanilla extract.
3. Add the buttermilk and mix until combined.
4. Add the dry ingredients and mix until just combined - make sure not to overmix.

5. Transfer the batter to a piping bag.
6. In a separate bowl, combine the ground cinnamon, brown sugar and crushed pecans.
7. Fill a greased doughnut pan halfway with the batter.
8. Sprinkle the sugar mixture onto the doughnuts, then top with another layer of batter.
9. Bake at 400F for 7 minutes.
10. Cool for 1 minute in the pan, then flip the pan over to remove the doughnuts and cool completely on a wire rack.

Glaze

1. Cream the cream cheese in a bowl with an electric mixer until fluffy.
2. Add the confectioner's sugar and milk and mix until combined.
3. Dunk the doughnuts into the glaze and transfer to a wire rack. Enjoy!

Tiramisu Donuts

We just transformed your favorite Italian dessert into a fluffy, cream cheese-stuffed doughnut perfect for breakfast ... or whenever.

Ingredients

Doughnuts

- 1/2 cup whole milk

- 2 tablespoons water
- 2 1/4 teaspoons active dry yeast
- 2 tablespoons sugar
- 3 tablespoons unsalted butter, melted and slightly cooled
- 2 large eggs + 1 large yolk
- 1 tablespoon espresso powder
- 2 1/2 cups all-purpose flour
- Vegetable oil, for frying

Tiramisu Cream

- 1 cup heavy whipping cream
- 1 1/2 cups powdered sugar
- 8 ounces cream cheese, softened
- 1 teaspoon vanilla extract

- 1/4 cup espresso, cooled to room temperature
- Topping: Grated dark chocolate and powdered sugar

Steps

Doughnuts

1. Heat milk and water until warm; stir in sugar and active yeast. Let it sit until mixture is foamy.
2. Pour the yeast mix into a stand mixer fitted with a paddle attachment.
3. Add melted butter, eggs and espresso powder.

4. With the stand mixer at low speed, add half of the flour. Change to hook attachment and add the rest of the flour. Continue to mix until a ball of dough comes together.

5. Transfer dough to oiled bowl, cover and rest for one hour.

6. Punch down dough, then turn out onto a floured surface.

7. Use a round cutter to cut doughnuts. Set aside to rest for 15 minutes.

8. Fill a large pot with vegetable oil. Heat to 350 degrees F.

9. Fry doughnuts for 75 seconds, or until they float. Flip and fry for another 60 seconds.

Remove and drain on a paper towel. Set aside to cool completely.

Tiramisu Cream

1. While the doughnuts are cooling, beat heavy whipping cream until you have stiff peaks. Chill until ready to use.
2. Mix powdered sugar and cream cheese until smooth.
3. Mix in vanilla extract and the espresso. Fold the whipped cream into the cream cheese mixture.

4. Transfer into a piping bag with a large tip. Pipe the tiramisu mix into the center of each doughnut.

5. Dust with powdered sugar and grate some dark chocolate on top. Enjoy!

Cat Doughnuts

We're paw-sitive you'll want these adorable cat doughnuts right meow.

Ingredients

- 1/3 cup + 1 tablespoon buttermilk
- 3 tablespoons unsalted butter, melted
- 1 cup all-purpose flour
- 1 teaspoon baking powder
- 1/4 teaspoon salt

- 1/4 cup sugar
- 2 tablespoons honey
- 1 large egg
- Almonds
- 3 tablespoons whipping cream
- 1 teaspoon vanilla extract
- 1 cup confectioner's sugar
- Food coloring

Steps

1. Whisk together the flour, baking powder and salt in a small bowl and set aside.
2. In a large bowl, combine the butter, sugar, honey, egg and vanilla extract. Add the buttermilk and mix until combined.

3. Spoon the batter into a greased doughnut pan.

4. Bake at 400F for 7 minutes.

5. Cool for 1 minute in the pan, then flip the pan over to remove the doughnuts and cool completely on a wire rack.

6. Make the glaze: Whisk together the whipping cream and vanilla extract. Add the confectioner's sugar and whisk until fully combined. Divide the glaze into as many bowls as you like, depending on the color you'd like your kitties to be.

7. Make sure to dye a small amount black, for the eyes and noses.

8. Slice small slits into each doughnut and stick an almond into each slit to look like cake ears.

9. Drizzle the glaze onto the doughnuts, creating spots or stripes as desired.

10. Use a toothpick to draw their faces with the black-colored glaze.

11. Allow the glaze to stiffen, about 20 minutes and enjoy!

Made in the USA
Monee, IL
06 December 2020